# When Boaz Doesn't Want Ruth

# Who is this book for?

Everyone who wants to do better.
Everyone who has made mistakes as a single person.
Everyone who wasn't quite sure what the standard is.
Everyone who needs to be reminded that your life and destiny has a
purpose.

---

# Dedication:

This book is dedicated to my parents who taught me by example the
power
of Boaz clinging to Ruth. You showed me firsthand, great marriages
are real. You were a blessing to one another and an example to all
your children. Your demonstration of Christian marriage has blessed
me and allowed me to be a blessing to others as I ministered to them
because I saw it done the right way!

I also thank my mother, Reverend Doctor Eleanor Cardenas
for living a life of holiness as a single woman after the death of my
father. Her example of holiness, her listening ear, prayers and godly
advice has blessed my life immeasurably and kept me out of A LOT
of trouble.

Whenever I fell short, she loved me back in order.

It is further dedicated to my friends, both married and single, who have held up my arms on the journey. Thank you. No one can walk this journey successfully in a vacuum.

# Introduction

Absolutely nobody that knows me would call me shy. The truth is, I am extremely introverted in many ways. As much as I say, and as much as I share both with the Kingdom and in secular arenas through lectures, speeches, sermons, and writings, I'm also very guarded in an effort to reduce the amount of offense surrounding certain issues. Well, today that comes to an end.

I have waited eight years to write this book in large part because I didn't want to be the one to write it. I didn't want to publicly address the foolishness that I see day in and day out amongst believers.

My other books have been Bible studies and devotional reflections, which made writing those texts easier. However, in writing *When Boaz Doesn't Want Ruth* I am stepping into a different realm; one in which I share personal thoughts, and perspectives that speak to the need of the people of God to behave as the people of God. In this hour of itching ears, whenever there is correction and a call for holiness, we open ourselves up for a different type of push back from those who are attempting to make this an ala carte religion.

How the *world* acts is absolutely NONE of my business. The world has its own set of rules, but as far as the church goes – it's for the Church to regulate the Church. We are responsible for our conduct and our adherence to scripture.

The Islamic mosque isn't taking its cues from the world, the Jewish Synagogue is not letting secular society dictate it's culture and beliefs – only Christians are so obsessed with political correctness and external acceptance that it bends, twists, deletes and violates its OWN written Holy book, the Bible, in order to make people who aren't even in the religion comfortable with those who are practitioners.

Holiness is right.

**"Make every effort to live in peace with everyone and to be holy;**
**without holiness no one will see the Lord."**
**Hebrews 12:14 NKJV**

No matter who falls short, or who messes up completely – the standard is holiness. Someone else's failure is no excuse for you or I to fail. We all have to press toward the mark.

**Brethren, I count not myself to have apprehended: but this one thing I do, forgetting those things which are behind, and reaching forth unto those things which are before, I press toward the mark for the prize of the high calling of God in Christ Jesus. Philippians 3:13-14**

At this point, I simply don't care who's upset about what I'm about to share - the Kingdom is in crisis. My job as a proclaimer of the gospel is not to amass crowds and garner "likes" on social media. If I don't get any thumbs and hearts anywhere but heaven – I promise you – I'm fine!

**"For the time will come when people will not put up with sound doctrine. Instead, to suit their own desires, they will gather around them a great number of teachers to say what their itching ears want to hear.**
**2 Timothy 4:3 NIV**

When Boaz (a saved man) Doesn't Want Ruth (a saved woman) he limits himself and calls into question the standards of the Kingdom. The Kingdom looks so much like the world until the world now views the Church as out of touch and irrelevant. Sadly, we have compromised our values so much that the world does not know where the church stands on principles that are foundational to our written doctrine.

Dating, engagement, sex and marriage are included in what I call, "New Gray Areas". "New Gray Areas" are areas in our faith and doctrine where we pretend not to know what is right. These are areas in which our opinions change every decade or so or are largely controlled by who the offender is, and what sins we need to overlook for our own benefit or the benefit of who we are covering for. There is an illogical, imbalanced and unbiblical view that if the people doing wrong are strangers, they are hell-bound but if they are leaders or our relatives and friends, we "shouldn't judge and God knows their hearts" Foolishness! If you chose not to live that standard that is 100% your choice. What is NOT your right is to try to change the tenants of the faith to accommodate your sin of choice.

What do you do when Boaz doesn't want Ruth? When butt injections trump brains and augmented breasts are valued above augmented spiritual lives what are we to do? What happens when Godliness no longer attracts many of the men who say they love God. What has become of us when holiness and faithfulness to God is a seldom noticed accessory rather than the celebrated garment? How are we as leaders setting a standard for men or women when the church freely marries under-counseled, uncounseled and unequally yoked people and holds no one accountable to their vows?

*When Boaz Doesn't Want Ruth* is not a heavy theological dissertation on the nuances of "all things relationship". It is however, an authentic reflection on the multi-layered issues surrounding dating, engagement and marriage among <u>believers</u>.

If you don't believe in Jesus, feel free to read the book and glean as much as possible. Jesus loves you and wants you to allow him into your heart. If you sense my frustration it's not with people who don't know the rules – it's with those who know them but ignore them while claiming to love and follow the One who gave them.

**"Whoever has My commandments and keeps them is the one who loves Me. The one who loves Me will be loved by My Father, and I will love him and reveal Myself to him." John 14:21**

To be clear, being single takes no effort. Singleness only requires not being married. The complexity of singleness comes as Christians seek to honor the standard of holiness and enact biblical principles in our everyday lives.

*"Being single as a Christian is only a challenge when you are trying to do it right."*

By the end of this first volume of a four-part series, I want you to walk away understanding another perspective on singleness. I am fully prepared for some to disagree with me, but I am writing for the masses of singles – male and female who I know will read this and breathe a sigh of relief because someone actually "gets it"!

My sole goal in writing is to provide the application and information to accompany the expectation. The church has been thorough in its instruction to singles to abstain. The church however, has completely failed to discuss *how* to implement the principles, *explain why* it is critical to adhere to the principles of holiness (beyond getting in heaven) or *provide true accountability* to safeguard the souls of the sheep. There are deep spiritual and natural consequences of our choices as singles.

While biblical principles stand in their fullness, much of the tension surrounding Christian dating comes from the unspoken issues, silent expectations, misunderstandings and sometimes outright bad theology attached to dating, relationship building, engagement, marriage and sex.

## Please Be Advised

This book is not for the sensitive or faint of heart. This book is also not for children. I am extremely straightforward, and I won't be sugar-coating things in this book.

The church universal has been sending coded messages about singleness, engagement, relationships and marriage but I have come to realize that there are some people who simply need to hear the truth and hear it plainly spoken.

I really toiled internally about how "real" I could keep it. I tried to dial it back to tell the truth while keeping it soft and palatable for the general church member who, in this hour, tends to be extremely oversensitive about any level of correction, rebuke or straight talk. This is an interesting level of selective sensitivity as many of these same people can also watch hours of vulgar and violent reality TV, listen to explicit music and watch movies that flat out show things we wouldn't even mention in past years....then we get to church and we have to act like we're in children's church to make sure that no one is offended. Life is short and souls have to take precedent over personal comfort.

As I discussed the stagnation I felt as I tried to write while carefully attempting to navigate these waters - and not being at peace with it - a dear friend looked at me and said, "then you may as well not even write the book because we are tired of books that don't just tell us how it is."

Thank you for holding me accountable sister.
Message heard. Crown adjusted.

It's about to go down.

*"Let's be clear, I didn't come to argue.
I came to teach."*

Roxanne Cardenas

RevTeaches.com

# TABLE OF CONTENTS

## CHAPTER 1: THE DANGER OF A BROKEN SYSTEM

## CHAPTER 2: A QUICK TOUR THROUGH THE BOOK OF RUTH

## CHAPTER 3: DATING 101

## CHAPTER 4: I'M NOT YOUR MAMA, YOUR BANK OR YOUR BABYSITTER!

## CHAPTER 5: WHY MARRIAGE MATTERS

WHY YOU CAN HAVE SEX ON SATURDAY: MARRIAGE IS COVENANT, NOT JUST
CONTRACT!
WATCH THE LOUSE WITH A SPOUSE
GRACE IS NOT A HALL PASS

## CHAPTER 6: A CHAPTER FOR THE HOES

DEAR HOE,
  HOMEWRECKING HOES
  CHURCH PROWLING HOES
  HYPOCRITICAL HOES
MALE HOES - I DIDN'T FORGET YOU!
THE HOE IN DENIAL: SO YOU THINK YOU'RE NOT A HOE...
HEAVEN AND THE HOE: THERE'S GOOD NEWS!

## CHAPTER 7: A QUICK MESSAGE FOR THE PEDOPHILES AND PREDATORS

YOU ARE WRONG. PERIOD
 BREAK THE CYCLE

## CHAPTER 8: JESUS WAS SINGLE: A FEW REMINDERS FROM THE SINGLES IN YOUR CHURCH

WE HAVE VALUE
WE HAVE LIVES
WE WANT TO BE INCLUDED AS EQUALS
  YOU ARE NOT MORE OF AN ADULT OR A CHRISTIAN BECAUSE YOU ARE MARRIED
  WE NEED CONTINUAL, SUPPORTIVE MINISTRY THAT ISN'T A MEAT MARKET

## CHAPTER 9: SO YOU THINK YOU FOUND THE ONE?

Before You Even Ask (BYEA)  Couple's Questionnaire.  - Foundational Questions to ask BEFORE you even ask!

# Chapter 1:
## The Danger of a Broken System

# The Danger of a Broken System

In biblical times the only way a man of faith could have sex, within accepted norms, was either to hire a prostitute or get married. If he used a prostitute, it made him unclean and temporarily separated him from God. After using a prostitute there were restrictions on his ability to go to the temple and to offer sacrifices. Men in that time understood that a moment of paid pleasure had prolonged, expensive and spiritual consequences. However, if he married, it gave him access to God-approved sex and the marriage was seen as another expected milestone in the journey of manhood.

There was no such thing as a random booty call among believers. Men knew that not only was casual sex forbidden, they were required by Mosiac law to pay the price for violating someone's daughter – and often had to marry her anyway! (Read Deuteronomy for details) In that biblical system there was no such expectation such as, "I bought her a nice steak, now she will sleep with me". That wasn't the system.

Women were taught to be virgins even to the point where it might cost them their lives if they did not keep their virginity until their marriage. (Deut. 22:21) The system was in place that women said "no", men knew not to ask, and they were able to function with the expectation that when men had a desire for a sex they knew they had to convince another man (the bride's father) or group of men the elders of the community) that he was man enough to handle the responsibility of taking care of a wife. The system didn't allow for a man to marry a woman when he had no job, no money, no shelter and no way to provide. Love wasn't enough. Cute wasn't enough! Sexy wasn't enough!

Men had to prove they were RESPONSIBLE in order to have access to a wife and thereby, have access to sex.

Why is that significant? God knew that a man was going to want sex! With the system the way it was, it forced a man to grow up if he ever wanted to be eligible to have sex that wasn't attached to a prostitute. A man was highly motivated to learn to provide. He had motivation to keep a good name and be the kind of man that could stand before a woman's father or the community at large and ask for a woman's hand. A young man also had to learn to be a good steward of money because he knew whoever he married – he would need to pay her dowry.

In modern times, because the sexual system is broken, many men feel that there is no need to get married when so many women are willing to do everything a wife does *without* the commitment or responsibility of marriage.

We have godly women struggling to find their place in a broken system.

There are women now who will pay a man's back child support, back taxes, do his laundry, cook, clean and meet all of his sexual needs and desires without any spiritual or legal commitment. Broken women in a broken system prefer a stagnant and incompetent man to having no man at all. These women will make excuses for a man who does not work. She will publicly defend her man who spends the day at home playing video games while she works two jobs and provides for the household. This is the kind of woman who says she doesn't want her man working in some fast food restaurant but will hand over her tax refund so he can sell drugs as if this was a more honorable occupation. When something happens, she doesn't have money for a lawyer or a casket – but she has lots of shoes, purses and bundles representing how well "Bae takes care of me".

Broken women will allow men to not only sleep with them, but sleep with others in what they call an 'open relationship'. We used to call it cheating. These women are so deluded that they consider being in an open relationship the epitome of transparency. They somehow convince themselves that if a man is sleeping primarily with them somehow that indicates his undying loyalty and commitment.

### Sis...lean in and let me tell you a secret.

A man can sleep with you and never, ever, EVA intend to speak to you again. A man, especially one who is not committed to God, can sleep with you without emotional attachment or any intention to pursue you further. A godless man will do godless things for some tail. He will lie, cheat, manipulate and spend money in order to secure a..."moment". Sexing you does not mean he loves you, cares about you or wants to build with you.

# Brothers...you're next...come here.

The best way to have no windows, no tires and a cell phone with 129 missed calls and 315 angry text messages is to make a woman think that you are in love when all you wanted was a chance to see how it is. A woman is not emotionally wired by God to have emotion free sex. Generally, if a woman is having sex with you while you are dating, she is anticipating either 1) securing a role in your life (becoming exclusive) or 2) advancing her role in your life (sifting from girlfriend to fiancée/wife). A woman with ANY modicum of self-esteem is not just our here giving out free samples! There is an intentionality – even to sin.

Men, when you meet a woman who has emotionless, no-strings attached, come-and-go as-you-please sex - **RUN.** Whether she knows it or not she is wounded in a way that has caused her to operate in a state of numbness that she thinks is protecting her. This is not who you want to sleep with and she is not who you want to play with. This kind of woman doesn't care about coming to your house, your job or our church causing a scene when you miss a payment. Whether that payment is attention, acknowledgement or cash a woman with a reprobate mind has nothing to lose by exposing you, extorting you or sending you through emotional and psychological warfare to make you pay for deeds done by other men in her past. Easy isn't always easy.

Isaiah 4:1 talks about the desperation of women who will provide their own clothes and food in exchange for a man's last name - yet as desperate as that is –even they demanded marriage.

Since the system is broken, many men don't find themselves rushing to solidify Godly relationships through marriage, they just keep moving through the process of singleness, often without including celibacy. When surrounded by so many easy options that require no commitment, it's easy to lose sight of the fact that while you are caught up in the pleasures of "Delilah" you have Ruths waiting alone looking at Boaz waste his strength. Sadly, by the time many men realize that they have engaged in pursuing the wrong type of woman that woman has intentionally created one or more institutional entrapments to stay connected to that man. Whether it's a baby, finances or access to his secrets the wrong woman will always find a way to make you pay for not selecting her

The system is already broken which is why the church cannot afford to be. As long as the church refuses to talk openly about sex, we are going to continue to see rate of HIV increase in the kingdom. We're going to continue to see diseases and other problems within the four walls of our local churches. We have to get over the stigma of sex and sexual conversation and begin to be courageous enough to address the fact that many of our members, young and old, are actively having unsanctioned sex while sitting in the pews clapping their hands and singing in worship. All of this is happening while many leaders claim to have open eye visions of houses, cars and increase but can't discern that a third of your church is headed to hell.

YES, great leaders, we have a role in this mess too. You are "so deep" that you act like you levitate at night when you pray but don't see that your tenors have prettier eyebrows than your soprano section and the praise team has NO OIL and your youth ministry is single handedly populating the church nursery? We MUST have serious conversations about sex at the local church level and we can't talk about sex if we are having sex with the people we need to be talking to about sex. Read that again – nice and slow.

# Don't Be a Rental

I don't know if you've ever rented a car for any length of time, but when you rent a car and you know you're going to have it for two weeks, a month, or two months - the truth of the matter is you drive it differently that you drive your regular car. It's not that you are reckless but subconsciously you just don't care on the same level because the car is not yours. You're not as careful about not hitting a curb. You don't swerve left and right trying to avoid potholes. You're not concerned when the oil light comes on because you don't have to change the oil. If something doesn't sound quite right, you don't panic because it's not your job to fix it. Afterall, the car is not yours. All you have to do is put a little gas in it and keep on driving to your heart's content, enjoying the ride.

Many times, rental cars come with unlimited mileage. The freedom of having no restrictions causes you to not even be concerned about the wear and tear, highway miles versus city miles, or anything else. Your only job is to...enjoy the ride. Every time we make sex just a ride that's exactly how we become in the eyes of others who are enjoying that ride.

When a man has no obligation to maintain you, care for you, shield you from bumps and bruises in the road of life, no obligation to maintain your life and lifestyle, to guard your heart, to shelter your spirit, to raise the children that he produces - all you are is a ride. He finds no need to be all the man he could be, because you've already reduced yourself to being less of a woman than God has called you to be.

Don't be a rental, because just like the car, once the fun is over and the thrill is gone the driver will turn you back in empty, dirty and with a bunch of miles on your engine and never look back.

# WHYYYYYYYY ARE YOU TALKING TO ME?

Have you ever been in a situation where you wonder why someone is talking to you? Imagine: You are sitting in your office minding your business and someone steps in your office flustered and angry and begins loudly complaining about other departments, other managers and other issues that you have no control of. They begin to list the many way things you need to change. They have you tap your neighbor – I mean email a coworker - and recommend changes that she should make even though she isn't the source of the problem either. How long would you let them talk? How long would you let them blame you for things that your department didn't even handle? How long before you sent them to the person who could solve the problem?

Imagine that person blamed you week after week about the issues of the other department. They continue to tell you to make change after change and try to convince you that the deficits in the other department would be solved if YOU made enough changes – even though it's not your department. Perhaps you are more spiritual than I, but at some point, I would have to speak up!

## "WHYYYYYYYY ARE YOU TALKING TO ME? GO TALK TO THE PEOPLE IN THE DEPARTMENT THAT MAKES THE DECISIONS!"

This is what is currently happening in the Church. Almost EVERY discussion about singleness is geared toward women. We aren't enough. We need to do better.

We need to change. We need to comb our hair in another direction. We need to cook less food that ends in "helper" ...I get it – we have to improve.

As we are the largest demographic in the church on Sunday, we catch the brunt of the lectures, but if the man is making the decision regarding who he marries because he is doing the "finding"...why are you talking to me?

When was the last time you heard men preached to about praying for the RIGHT wife? Name the men's conference that had breakout sessions for single men to tell them the 25 reason's they still don't have a wife. Name the sermon where men were shamed for being single. Enough with the single shaming of women. Go talk to the decision makers. Go talk to the men and encourage them in how they can make better choices. Tell THEM what to look for. Share with THEM strategies for celibacy...or is that just a requirement for women in the Kingdom? The Kingdom is responsible for educating and empowering MEN with the same passion and intensity it uses as it speaks to women. Leaders, build men up until their standards are so high that women HAVE TO line up with the Word to even be noticed by a saved man, let alone married to one.

If you want to see Kingdom women change, stop glorifying women who don't reflect the standard of holiness.

# Men of God, We Need You!

Just a quick personal note to the men of God.
We need you.

I know that there is a movement of women who boast that they don't need a man for anything because men are unnecessary and obsolete. I'm not here to argue that they are bald-faced, bitter liars with other issues that I don't have time in this edition to get into, because that would be mean. What I will say is that men play a very important role in the life of a woman. How that role is played affects a woman consciously and subconsciously all of her life. It affects her choices, her tone, her confidence, her openness to people and yes, how she sees herself sexually.

A man is the protector, defender and provider for the woman. That woman may be his wife, mom, grandmother, aunt, sister, cousin, niece or sister in Christ - but he matters in different ways in each role.

Biblically there was no such thing as a woman waking up one day deciding she wanted her own tent and to build a life by herself for herself. There was ALWAYS a man assigned to her, assuring that she would be well cared for. Book by book in the Bible you see men protecting, loving and shielding different women in their lives. When a man harmed a woman, he had to answer to other men who would deal with him accordingly.

**Men we need you and we love you.**

We need you to know your own value. We want you to love yourself in a healthy way and to let that love overflow in how you love us. I know we can be difficult. Although it seems much easier, being a woman in our society has significant challenges. We aren't paid equally, viewed equally, respected equally or protected equally. For some, the difficulties create walls that make us appear abrasive and rude. In truth, many of my sisters are just trying to self- protect because someone, somewhere failed to be the man that perhaps you are – or are striving to be. So, when you see us looking "mean" at the gas station, sometimes it's because looking "friendly" isn't always safe. Say hello anyway. Open the door anyway. Keep your eyes above our ears as you do so. That helps us feel respected. (If you have to look, you can look when we're not looking at you looking at us – but remember, no stares, touches or disrespectful comments...that's creepy and again, makes us feel unsafe which only reinforces the "mean" wall.)

I know that we pretend that we have everything under control. We don't. Your role in our lives is essential and I can personally attest to the fact that my own life has been immeasurably enhanced by Godly men who took their role in my life seriously and chose (because it is a choice) to make a positive and safe place for me in different seasons of my life.

Men of God, be great. Be great when you think no one's looking, caring or is concerned. With or without applause, be the BEST you can be. We need you to have integrity and not just persona. Persona is who you portray yourself to be publicly, while your character speaks to the essence of your integrity when no one is looking at you, rewarding you or acknowledging you.

### You all are leaders. LEAD.

You stepping your game up forces us to do the same. Some of the mess you see among women is because MEN won't stand up and say something. We need you to be the voice of reason in a chaotic world who will support the women who want to be modest and yet appreciated. We need you to be a big brother to a sister and not keep quiet while a wolf devours her. We need you to not to victimize the women who market themselves as easy. No real hunter buys gear and gets dressed up to take aim at a deer that's already been hit by a car. When something is available but too easy it takes the thrill out of the pursuit – at least for a real hunter. Men, learn to see that woman with no boundaries or standards as a wounded a deer – not a prized gazelle.

Forgive us for the times we didn't get you. Forgive us for the times we ignored your pain and stated or implied that simply because you are a man you didn't have a right to express a full spectrum of feelings and emotions.

We are working on ourselves too. Pray for us, we are certainly praying for you!

# THE GENDER HYPOCRISY

**Be ye not unequally yoked together with unbelievers: for what fellowship hath righteousness with unrighteousness? And what communion hath light with darkness? 2 Corinthians 6:14**

The church often talks about the importance of being equally yoked. 'Equally yoked' is an agricultural reference that speaks to two animals of the same side and strength being paired together. As they do the work to which they are assigned they're able to work effectively together. If one gets tired, the other one has the capacity to lift the load and carry it and vice-versa. Since they are similar in size and strength, one does not bear more of the load than the other, but they are fit to pull together to get the job done and so when we talk about being equally yoked in the body of Christ, the scripture is clear – believers are not to marry unbelievers. We are pretty good about communicating this verbally although, to our shame, seldom will we refuse to do a wedding for this reason yet if there is ever a reason to decline this would be in the top three.

What we do not share as readily is that you can have two Christians and they still not be truly compatible. Just because you both love Jesus doesn't mean you should build a life together. The question becomes, is the person you're with or considering for marriage of the same spiritual size and strength as you? Are you all paired together in a way that is nearly-equal or is one significantly stronger than the other? When times get tough will there be an uneven distribution of the spiritual workload? How long can the stronger person bear the load without getting tired, frustrated and bitter.

The hypocrisy comes in when women are berated and taken through all manner of changes every time they attempt to date someone who is growing in Christ. People will quickly say to a woman, "he's not ready" and "it will never work". Conversely, I have watched men in leadership marry unsaved women and have people who are seasoned in church look at them and say, "just keep working with her, she'll get there".

As a woman in ministry, if whoever I'm dating doesn't know how to break down the Talmud and the translate the Septuagint and know the locations of the missing parts of the Dead Seas Scrolls people look upside my head like I have backslid.

Huh? So women need to marry strong believers but men don't? The gender-based hypocrisy only reinforces 1) bad decision making for men and 2) perfection-based pickiness among women. Too many women will pass up a great man because he isn't dressed like one the original twelve disciples and doesn't answer the phone in tongues.

We all have flaws and room to grow. God isn't looking for us to bring perfect potential spouses to the table, but at least people who are comparable to us in our faith walk and journey. Both men and women need to ask the question: Are we equally yoked? Women must ask,

"Does this man love God, does he love me and is He in a position to lead our home well?

Men need to ask, "Is this woman saved and able to manage the affairs of our home and teach our children the foundational principles of the faith while serving as an equal partner"?

The church is loud in its correction and demands of women while standing silently by when men make bad choices based on her boobs and booty. Men, if you think your destiny is going to be fulfilled because of somebody's lips, hips, and fingertips, you don't have good sense and chances you really are not ready to be married. It's 2019! You can buy cute, but you can't buy character!

The hypocrisy of the church which stands back and lets its sons make bad decisions just because it is filling a sexual need for the moment is reprehensible. If you look through the word of God, most men that were brought down were brought down behind a piece of tail and we don't want to talk about that. We don't want to discuss the fact that many times after a man has slept with a woman the soul tie is so strong that it can cause that man to make a bad temporary decision a bad decision for a lifetime. The Bible says in Proverbs 18:22, "He that finds a wife finds a good thing and obtain a favor from the Lord".

Man of God, does the person you want to marry reflect a God-sized level of favor? *Not flavor,* **FAVOR.**

Is this the person that is assigned to help meet your destiny and your goals?

Is this the person of character, quality and compassion that can help you raise a family or build an economic empire or do great exploits in ministry or just be a better man?

Many times, after it's all said and done, people step back and reflect on the fact that they made a decision based on their eyes and not their journey. I'm not telling anybody to marry somebody that you don't find attractive, but I'm saying that if cute is all they have and if they are sitting on their best asset -you are about to make a critical error sir.

**Chapter 2:**

**A QUICK TOUR THROUGH THE BOOK OF RUTH**

The story of Boaz and Ruth is a love story for the ages for many reasons. When you ask many churched, single, women what they are hoping and waiting for – "her Boaz" may be in the top few responses.

Interestingly there are many nuances about the story that we do not discuss. Let's speed walk through the book of Ruth. I highly encourage you to take the time to read Ruth. It's only 4 chapters but a powerful four chapters they are.

**Ruth Chapter 1**: In chapter one we find a family experiencing a crisis. There was a famine in Bethlehem where they lived. The family, consisting of Elimelek, Naomi and their two sons Mahlon and Kilion went to the town of Moab to live there. Elimelek died and Naomi kept it moving with boys. Both sons got married. One had a wife named Orpah and the other had a wife named Ruth. After living there 10 years both the sons died leaving Naomi with no husband, no sons and two women she couldn't support. Naomi is heartbroken as you would imagine and tells both women to go back 1) to their homes and 2) to their gods. This indicates that both had left their former way of life as Moabites and converted when they were married. Orpah left Ruth stayed. When Naomi got to town, she had to look bad because the people in her hometown didn't recognize her and her return caused quite a stir. Naomi is grieving and feeling that the Lord has forsaken her. Things aren't looking good. Luckily the barley harvest was beginning.

**Ruth Chapter 2:** Boaz was a member of her deceased husband's family so Naomi trusted that he, as a man and relative of sorts, would look out for her and at least keep her safe as a widow, who now has no sons. Ruth offered to go grab the leftovers of the harvest that were left on the ground after the barley was collected. This was a system set up to help the poor. Ruth heads to the field and the field belongs to Boaz! Ruth had to be fine because even sweaty from working all day Boaz asked his employees who she was. He then offered her placement, protection and provision. He offers her attachment free help and she returns home to tell Naomi all that has happened only to have Naomi share that Boaz was actually family. Ruth worked all season in safety because a man told the other men not to bother her.

Note* He did not try to sleep with her. She did not offer him a special 'thank you' for looking out because times were tough. She bowed and he pronounced a blessing over her life because of her works and character. Her "fine" was the frosting, not the cake. A woman of character is the total package.

**Ruth Chapter 3**: At the end of the season Naomi tells Ruth she needs to find her a husband and she suggests Boaz. She tells Ruth to cute it up and head in there! Ruth does and makes it clear she wants to be his wife. She does not sleep with him as some would try to suggest. In fact, Boaz says, "Hey there is a guy ahead of me to claim you first and if he wants to – so be it" which would be the last thing a woman wants to hear after sex. He speaks to character and the community's opinion of her. He gives her more provisions and promises to resolve the matter quickly.

Ruth Chapter 4: Boaz makes arrangements with the elders to secure Ruth. Boaz keeps the conversation centered around the piece of land and when the man is interested, he adds that he would have to take the widow (Ruth, a major expense) with the land. The man passes. Boaz gets Ruth! Boaz and Ruth get married and Ruth gets pregnant! Naomi cares for the baby and people said it was as if Naomi got another son! Life was redeemed for ALL of them!

## It's all about perspective

Now here is the juicy part. Boaz's mama is Rahab. Yup. THAT RAHAB. Rahab the former prostitute from Jericho. Rahab helped the Israelites and in exchange the soldiers didn't kill her and her family. Rahab and her family were set outside the camp because they were not part of the people of God. Something had to happen...something we don't know the fullness of because not only is Rahab married to an Israelite named Salmon she is the mother of Boaz (Matthew 1 and Ruth 4) and listed in Hebrews 11 among the great people of faith!

Boaz knew firsthand that God can transform a prostitute and God can transform. Boaz had Obed and Obed was Jesse and Jesse was the father of David. Yes, KING David! Boaz made a choice the flowed all the way to Jesus!

## When Boaz wants Ruth generations are impacted and great things happen.

It is possible that seeing this woman raised in a pagan community, who had converted upon marriage reminded him of his own mother's journey. He didn't see her as less than. He didn't see her nationality or her sexual past. He saw her for her current relationship with God, her mother in law and her display of character! Boaz wanted Ruth! He wanted integrity, he wanted a hard worker – and yes, I'm sure she was cute.

What happens when some of our modern day Boazes seem to find modern day Ruth's undesirable? What do homes look like when we celebrate "baby daddies" over husbands and "baby mamas" over wives?

## What does the Kingdom look like when Boaz doesn't want Ruth?

What happens when Ruth is seen as too boring and independent? Biblical Ruth preferred to work for her wheat and not "sleep for it".  To the biblical Boaz that was admirable but for some today that it may be challenging to appreciate purity when so many others, even within the chuch, present low-hanging fruit. We must deal honestly with dating, relationships, engagement, marriage and sex in order to support single people in their journey to live lives that are pleasing to God and beneficial to their collective journeys.

The following chapters are just a primer into the deeper conversation we will have further into the series.  Grab a highlighter and mark this book up! Use these chapters as talking points at church, work and among friends. We cannot lose another generation of "Boazes and Ruths" to bad relationships and carnality.


Let's start with dating!

# Chapter 3:
# DATING  101

# Why we date

**Ya'll!  Date to socialize, survey and have fun!**

Leaders, please stop telling people the only reason to date is to get married. This is why church people sit at the house in a spiritual bubble getting nothing accomplished. When they finally go out, they're so desperate and thirsty, they do the first thing that hops into their mind when they go on their little date.

 The best thing to do is to go out just to have good, clean fun!  When you go out to have a good time you remove the pressure of every date being "the one"!  Keep in mind, the definition of a good time for a Christian is different than the definition of a good time for a non-Christian.

> *Saints, we're not going to the hotel to Netflix and chill for "a good time".
> *We don't go to the strip club for "a good time".
> *We don't get drunk and high for "a good time" because it impairs our judgement and leads us to do everything our flesh contemplated doing in our sober mind.

Go to the movies, host a BBQ, walk in the park – please, go live your life and enjoy yourself. As you date and have a good time you'll begin to find people who you may want to have a second date, or a continued series of dates with. After some time, you may discover that you have found someone that you would like to consider as a potential mate. You cannot find a potential mate only dating once a year when you think you have found the perfect person that's already a candidate for marriage.

**Stop sitting at home trying to be deep, go out and date.**

## Why We Get Engaged

I encourage couples to do *pre-engagement* counseling because too often once a ring is purchased and family and friends are notified very seldom do people opt to back out – even when they know they should. Once the engagement is public, the attention tends to quickly shift to the details of the wedding and not the institution of marriage. Pre-engagement counseling allows couples to make a solid decision to move forward with a new level of confidence in their compatibility or provides them with a way to quietly separate without public interference or judgment.

When couples are dating seriously and exclusively (pre-engaged), they may share things such as salaries, debts, medical conditions and other issues that would not be casually discussed in general dating. Many of these intense and open discussions help clarify if they should move to the next step – engagement.

**Engagement** is the public acknowledgment of the private decision to get married. It is the way we notify friends, family and other potentially interested parties that we are officially "off the market" and no longer looking to explore our options with other people. Engagement, in its most effective form, is a commitment that is time-stamped with a wedding date.

"Engagement" was never meant to be a nebulous term used to clear a couple to live together and have unlimited sex since "they are getting married anyway". Engagement is not sexual layaway where you able to take your selection off the market and make small payments while enjoying the knowledge that "it's not going anywhere".

Engagement is a focused time where the couple should be intentional about learning all they can about themselves, one another, and the responsibilities and commitment of marriage. Engagement is a time to fully "engage" and put all of your cards on the table in a way you may not - and probably should not- when you are casually dating.

## What We're <u>Not</u> Gonna Do...

If you, like me, have endured countless "Single's Seminars" at various church conferences and retreats you probably have heard some of the most absurd advice that can be given to adult singles. Apart from being the friends of the hosts, I am unsure how some of our presenters are selected. Many of them quickly admit, as they prepare to teach a room full of singles on the cusp of 2020, that they have been married for 40 or 50+ years and were married at 20 or 23 which means they were only single as adults from 18-20 or 18-23.

Wow, you survived five years as a single adult and four years of that you weren't celibate...let me grab my pen to take notes – or not.

Let me be clear, there is absolutely nothing wrong with being a married person presenting to single people! However, you must be an informed and realistic presenter. You need to look at your audience and recognize their needs and struggles. Don't minimize the difficult task of being single and celibate (which is WAY different than just being single) and honor the journey they are on with real solutions to real situations.

I recently listen to a teaching in which one person said, "the same thing that worked in 1990 will work today". BABY BYE! Yes, prayer, fasting and holiness are enduring principles, but if you haven't been single since you had to lick a stamp and carry a ten-pound cell phone in a pouch over your shoulder I need you to at least admit that things are **NOT** the same as they were 20, 30 or 50 years ago.  Here are just **some** of the many ways that times *are* different:

- **Porn is free**. People used to pay for porn, now it's free which makes it more accessible and more of an issue, and at times an addiction, for some.
- **TV has a mind of its own.** TV used to shut off at midnight with the Star Spangled Banner, now after midnight TV turns into porn and plastic penis sales – and you don't need cable to see sex scenes anymore. (Cartoons are sexually active too now.)
- **Steaks and Penises are for sale in the same place**. Sex toys used to be stigmatized, mail ordered or isolated to sex shops, now vibrators and massage oils are in every grocery store and pharmacy.

- **Sexual experimenting is encouraged**. Schools are teaching children that all forms of sex and sexuality are absolutely fine and they should partake in any form of sexual expression they want to, whenever "they" feel they are ready. (ie. Children as young as four are able to decide they should switch genders.)

- **People can pee whenever their emotions lead them.** Gender is perceived by some as fluid. People are able to go in whatever bathroom best represents their feelings on any given day.
- **Cheating now has different levels of social acceptability**. In the unchurched world people view cheating on a spectrum. What was called Adultery is now called being 'open, accepting, polyamorous and playful'.

That being said, here are some of the things I need presenters, pastors and teachers to **STOP** telling singles:

1. **Temptation is a sin.** Jesus was tempted. All God asked us <u>to do not was give in</u> to the temptation.
2. **When you get the infilling of the Holy Ghost you won't even want to do certain things.** You can have the Holy Ghost, speak in a thousand tongues, be at church every service and roll under every pew in the whitest of white sheets and you will STILL have to battle your flesh to line up with the word of God.
3. **God is your husband**. Jesus take the wheel! If ever a segment of scripture was stretched beyond recognition this is surely in the top 10. Let me say this loud and clear. Your daddy tucks you in, your husband gets in with you. There is a distinct and profound difference! God is your FATHER, not your lover.

4. **If you aren't married (as a woman) it's because you aren't ready or haven't done something right**. Stop using this ignorance to throw women into pits of despair, self-doubt and condemnation because they have not married yet. Some of the women you are condemning aren't being found because you told them to only go on dates with someone they would marry after two appetizers and a movie.

5. **You should only date in groups**. This advice is wonderful if you are 16 but it is a very bad idea when you are older and want to have a conversation to know the other person on an intimate (not sexual) level. If you think I'm about to tell you the depth of my heart in front of your mother, two cousins and your friends from Purity Circle #3 you are sadly mistaken. If your flesh is so tempted that you need 4-7 chaperones, not only are you not ready to marry – you aren't ready to date!

6. **"Sex isn't all that! - You aren't missing much."** If you don't sit your married self down! Baby if your testimony is that "sex isn't all that" I need you to stop lecturing me, be seated and gather yourself, your spouse and a few books and fix your horizontal ministry immediately! Sex is all that and then some - and to try to tell adults, many of whom have had sex, that sex is no big deal is condescending and silly. Say how

wonderful sex is...it's just not for singles! I told one married person who made a similar statement to me that her saying that to me was like someone full off an unlimited buffet telling someone dying of malnutrition that food is overrated. While I know that celibacy does not cause death, although it may feel that way from time to time, we ought not minimize the joy of amazing marital sex.

While this foolishness is being spread there is critical information that is NOT being shared.

1. **People need to talk about sex and body changes beyond puberty.** A whole lot happens between your period starting and having hot flashes or wet dreams and potential prostate enlargement. Churches need classes to discuss these changes including the hormone surges, reproductive health and Christian sexual education.
2. **There is no shame in seeking therapy.** If someone has suffered abuse in any form going to therapy should be suggested, supported and normalized.
3. **Singles are not second-class citizens.** Many churches do not have structured activities or consistent ministries for single members. Single members need to be supported and treated as equals.

# Chapter 4:
## I'M NOT YOUR MAMA, YOUR BANK OR YOUR BABYSITTER

The rules for dating as a Christian are vastly different than the rules for those who do not name Christ as Lord and Savior. That being said, what people who are unsaved may have told you about dating relationships and the opposite sex may be grossly different than what I'm about to share. What I'm about to share is critical for believers to understand because there is a standard as to how we handle the dating process and our expectations of one another through the process. So many of these standards have either been lost or interwoven between the sacred and secular that it has created great misunderstanding and the collapse of respect and boundaries. These boundaries help people to understand themselves and one another in a more excellent way and they must be re-established.

### It's not your job to raise the person you are dating

It's important for both men and women to remember that it is not your job to raise the person you're dating. If somebody comes into a relationship with a marked level of immaturity, God has not assigned you to raise them into the man or woman they're supposed to be. That is the job of their parents or pastor! Many times, the reasons that breakups hurt so badly is because we have heavily invested in immature people. We have helped to correct behaviors, change lifestyles, improve their overall being and enhance their life's journey only to have them betray us or treat us in a way that is not befitting of all of the investment of time, energy, and effort that we have put into them.

When we commit to helping to raise an immature person into who we think we really want or need, we are fooling ourselves into believing that we can "create" an equal. If you look at an adult that you would like to date or possibly marry, if you have to raise them, which means you must help them get from a place of total immaturity and lack of preparation for their life and life's goals, that very well may not be the person for you. We are not called to raise the people that we're going to be in covenant with.

When people are really called to be with us, while they grow, mature and become a better version of themselves we have to remember it is not our job to raise them. It is not our job to create the person of our dreams.

### It's not your job to fund the person you are dating

No matter who you are or who you are dating, it is not your job to fund them.

**Women:** Men are not ATM machines. Too many women in the Kingdom have become low-level whores. You can be mad at me for saying it if you want to, but if when you come short on a bill, need your hair done, need your toes and your fingers touched up, and your first thought is "What man can I call?" you have the same mentality as a worker on the street who sells herself for the essentials. We tend to look down on a prostitute because she is selling herself outright, but if you are doing things relationally, sexually or otherwise in exchange for gifts, services, rent, cars, car notes, or cash, you too are selling your services. Don't prostitute yourself.

**Young Ladies**: I need you to know that you are worth more than a $17 shrimp dinner at Red Lobster. If a man offered you $17 for sex you would be appalled, but too many of you will let a man take you Olive Garden and you end up giving him more than unlimited breadsticks should EVER be able to provide. Don't turn a trick for a Cheddar Bay biscuit. Men, I need you to use some common sense and ask yourself how many miles is on the engine of a woman who will sleep with you for a lobster tail and a margarita.

If someone exploited your mom, sister or daughter you would be livid! If your thought is, "if she's dumb enough to do it, I'm going to let her" then you need to consider your own level of wisdom and personal integrity – or lack thereof. To prey on the weak makes you weak and puts you in the same exploitive, manipulative category as your average street pimp.


**Sisters of all colors and creeds**, it is not a man's job to pay your household bills when you're dating. It is not a man's job to rescue you financially. It is not a man's job to pay for messes that he did not create, and likewise as women we have to be wise enough to understand it is not your job to fund, or fix, his life.

**Women**: Why are you paying his child support? Why are you paying for his financial errors? Why is he driving your car and not driving a car of his own? We have to start taking control of how we handle our financial lives and responsibilities. Part of what makes breaking up so difficult for many people is that they have interwoven their finances after they have moved in together, cosigned on loans and never got married. It becomes very difficult to divide things in a reasonable and sensible way without it becoming emotional and sometimes very dangerous. Keep your money to yourself until you're married. Don't cosign, don't work buy something together. Don't open up businesses together, unless you're able to work together without any attachment whatsoever, and for most people once they are emotionally connected, let alone sexually intimate, they are not able to make that clean break at the end of a relationship.

## Friends: If you see something, say something

Years ago, after 9/11, a security slogan became popular that simply said, "If you see something, say something." This same slogan can be put into full affect as it relates to relationships. If you are my friend, my full expectation is that you would tell me if you see an area of concern. If you see something, say something. That doesn't mean you're right and it doesn't mean that I'm going to make a decision regarding who I'm dating or who I'm engaged to solely based on your observation. However, you being honest *does* mean that somebody who may care about or love me, is looking at the situation from a different vantage point.

Friends may very well give some advice that is going to possibly help address the situation before it becomes a problem. Even better, your honesty may provide a safe space to acknowledge problems and search for a solution. You are not a good friend if you stand silently by and watch your friend end up with somebody who is absolutely wrong for them and is causing harm to their life, their spirit, their finances or their mental well-being. One of the worst things you can ever do is to have plenty to say to everyone else about the situation while failing to have the courage of your convictions to speak directly to the person that you are concerned about.

If you are worried about how their behavior has changed or are concerned for their personal safety - tell them directly. Don't call other people or post a non-descript, passive aggressive post on Facebook. Have the courage to address it friend to friend. If you're really a friend, "if you see something, say something."

**Chapter 5:**
**WHY MARRIAGE MATTERS**

### Why Marriage Matters

We have become a wedding obsessed culture. We love the allure of shows like, "Say yes to the Dress" and "Four Weddings". We love the buzz and hype of planning a wedding day while giving little to no thought to the marriage. Too often people select mates based on who they feel is sexy, rich or "full of potential" rather than who they believe is able to walk with them through the journey of life that God has assigned.

If you are a pro athlete and avid sports enthusiast, you probably shouldn't marry someone who hates sports. Likewise, if you are a Christian with a strong relationship with God why marry someone who doesn't even go to church? While it certainly doesn't mean they are a bad person, it may indicate that they are a bad person for you!

Singles, we spend far too much time while dating finding out people's favorite color and other meaningless, cutesy information that in no way bares any real relevance to the viability of a marriage. No one in the history of the world has stood in divorce court seeking a dissolution of marriage because they can't agree on who's favorite color is best. We need to be asking real-life, hard-hitting questions that allow us to be open and honest and hear the heart of the other person BEFORE we venture into a marriage.

Marriage matters because it is the only relationship on earth that is designed to parallel the relationship between Jesus Christ and his bride, the Church. When you're trying to imitate an established relationship, you then have an obligation to imitate it in its fullness. This means that the way the groom, Christ, behaves should be reflected in the way a groom treats his bride in a natural marriage. The same way The Church is supposed to be loyal and dedicated to Christ, should be how a bride in the natural treats her husband. That's why we know that if a man loves his bride the way Christ loved the church, it would be easy for a woman to lavish all of the respect and kindness back on the man.

Marriage matters because it is a symbol to the world reflecting what true covenant and true commitment look like. When people see that reflection, it should help them to be able to see the loving commitment that Christ shows to us.

The marriage statistics, even among believers, are abysmal. Making matters worse are the spineless members of the clergy who marry anyone who asks. There is never an excuse to marry someone who you have not counseled. When preachers treat marriage casually people will certainly do the same! Striking casual covenants should be considered malpractice and grounds for losing your license. When I stand to do a wedding, I am literally asking God to bless the union of the two people before me.

In saying this I understand God blesses things that are aligned with his WORD, not our emotions. If the relationship doesn't hold up biblically how can I ask God to bless it?

Preachers, don't be so desperate for a quick buck that you intentionally commit spiritual fraud by even giving the impression that God is in some of these insane extended hook ups we call marriages. We have a responsibility to keep the sacred - sacred and that which is holy - holy. We have no business marrying people to their pimps, mistresses or abusers.

It is 100% ok to tell a couple, "NO, I will not marry you". Further, if you are not their pastor, you need to have the fortitude to ask why the couple is asking you to do the service instead of their local pastor. Ask questions and keep asking because you are putting your ministerial seal of approval on this marriage by preforming the ceremony. Respect God and yourself enough not to make weddings your hustle.

I have included at the close of this book a copy of my premarital counseling booklet. Please feel from to buy copies of this book for couples and use it as a guide to prepare couple for the honest conversations needed to build a firm foundation for a marriage. I also host trainings for clergy to be more effective in pre-marital counseling and preparing people for marriage. People need to know that the wedding is the easy part, being married is where the real work takes place.

# Why you can have Sex on Saturday: Marriage is Covenant, Not Just Contract!

Many times, couples will get married on the weekend. They signed their marriage license and that marriage license is not even mailed to the courthouse for days. Nobody, and I mean NOBODY, waits to have sex until they get the official license from the city confirming that their license has been received and approved. The reason you can have sex on Saturday if you got married on Saturday is because the church considers your marriage the covenant that you stood before God and made. We recognize that marriage for the Christian, is both covenant and contract. The contract covers the natural side which helps to ensure the rights and legalities of this world -but the covenant speaks to the things of the spirit.

The promise for lifelong integrity, faithfulness and loyalty and all of the sacrificial extensions of love that God asked for us to do are not part of a contract of this world. It is the covenant that causes us to live right, be right, do right and extend ourselves beyond our self-centered comfort and our personal opinions, to do the will of God and to honor Hm through our marriage. It is essential you know your marriage is not just a contract. It is not just some paper you sign. It is not just some inconsequential document. It is the public acknowledgement that you have made in agreement with another human being and the God of your creation to be your absolute best for Him and for that other person and to allow that relationship to be the earthly illustration of the love, care and closeness of Christ and His Bride.

**WATCH THE LOUSE WITH THE SPOUSE**

If you tell me that you love the person that you're with, but you constantly cheat on them, and you live in ways that are disheartening and cruel emotionally to them, I have to question your love. While you may have a lot of great qualities, your ability to mistreat someone you saw you loves sends off red flags! If I get into business with you, I can know that I'll be treated in a way that is lesser than your spouse and rightfully so. Your spouse should have precedent over a business relationship, but if you are mean, surly and unkind to someone you say you love, what kind of behavior should I expect as someone who is going to be treated in a lesser fashion?

Whenever I see a louse with a spouse, I already know how to guard myself from that person. Stop expecting people who can dishonor their marriage to turn around and honor you in life and business. Any time somebody has gathered all of their friends, family, a minister, and spent thousands upon thousands of dollars to have a wonderful wedding to marry someone only to turn around casually and unapologetically bring disgrace and dishonor to that covenant -you can be assured that there is a high probability you will be treated by that person in an even worse manner.

### Grace is not a hall pass.

A few years back, there was a movie called *Hall Pass*. In the movie, a wife allows her husband to cheat for a set period of time with no consequences. The Hall Pass was acknowledgement that although cheating would take place the other person would not hold it against the offender. Many times, people consider the grace of God a hall pass! They could not be more wrong! Just because God doesn't kill you when you do something doesn't mean that He approves of it.

Any relationship where you do the wrong thing just because the love of the other person won't let them abandon you in the midst of your foolishness is not a functional relationship. There are people who think, "Obviously, He's not that mad about what I am doing because I'm still blessed." Honey, just because God doesn't expose every wrong that you do does not mean that God is not concerned or upset! The fact that God loves you and extends his mercy and grace to you is in no way a sign that he is okay with you doing whatever you want to do, when you want to do it, how you want to do it, and with whomever you want to do it. Grace is not a hall pass! It is the opportunity to get it right before He has to embarrass you to get your attention.

# Chapter 6:

# A Chapter For the Hoes

# A CHAPTER FOR THE HOES

Now I understand that for some people they may find the title offensive. But the Bible even says that women of low moral standards were called 'whores'. Men were referred to as "whoremongers" and an entire nation was guilty of "a whoring after other gods" (Judges 2:17) In fact there are 65 references to whores, whoredom and a whoring! I just took a couple letters off and shortened it to 'hoes' but either way if you're upset right now, and you feel some kind of way, chances are you need to read the whole chapter.

I'm fat. So, if people are talking about skinny people, I don't have any reaction because I'm not skinny, never have been, maybe never will be. At the end of the day, if it doesn't apply to you, get out your emotions. But if you're feeling emotional right now, you're probably the very person that needs to read through this.

Secondly, many times people only read certain portions of a book rather than the entire book cover to cover. So, I wanted to make it easy for the hoes to find the chapter that talked about them. I didn't want to weave it into the other chapters. I didn't want to send a little subliminal message. We've simply got to deal with the epidemic of whoredom sweeping the land. We can no longer afford to mince words and sugarcoat things so that people don't think that we're talking about them when in fact we are most certainly talking about them.

So, this chapter is specifically for the hoes. Moving on.

# Homewrecking Hoes

Now, there are different types of whorishness and I want to address a few kinds today. First, the homewrecking hoes. See, back in the day someone who was degrading themselves as a mistress understood their role was to be that partner in sin. They would know to be quiet, to be discreet, to be subtle. Now, these new hoes will ring your doorbell, call your phone, want to fight you in Aisle 9 in Wal-Mart and get mad at you because you don't want *them* sleeping with *your* husband.

Televised celebrity sin in the mainstream affects people's beliefs and values especially as it comes to the interpretation and acceptance of foolishness. Bill Clinton tried to convince a nation oral sex wasn't sex even though it has sex in its name. Then the mistresses of Tiger Woods tried to bamboozle the nation into believing that mistresses are victims.

Tiger Woods' mistresses got ya'll messed up! I stood in utter disbelief as a cadre of women – with an attorney – held a press conference to discuss how they had been wronged. I turned the volume up because SURELY the hoes haven't gathered with legal representation to complain that while sleeping with someone else's husband they were misled and deceived. You slept with a man you knew was married. You snuck around and had sex with a man who wasn't yours legally or spiritually and now…tissue in hand, you want to be the victim. No Ma'am. You're a homewrecking hoe. There was a <u>home</u>, your behavior helped <u>wreck it</u> because you, along with your sexual partner in crime, were being <u>hoes</u>.

I can hear the ignorant hoes in the back… "If his wife had been…."

Hefa, don't tell me anything about how "if she was doing her job he wouldn't be over here". You sound stupid. That's the exact same thing as saying if McDonalds made fried shrimp people wouldn't be at Red Lobster. HUH? McDonalds doesn't need to fry shrimp to make you eat there – you need to make your final purchase where they are serving what you want in the first place. If you didn't want to be married, DON'T GET MARRIED!

You wanted fried shrimp but went to McDonalds and got a Big Mac who is to blame? Now Red Lobster snuck you some fishy fried shrimp out the back door and suddenly "McDonalds wasn't what you thought it was."

Homewrecker, they selected what THEY wanted, gathered all of their friends and family and promised GOD that they would be faithful. Now after getting what THEY selected, you slither over into the situation and then blame her for his lack of integrity. No. Nope. Not today!

Oh...I hear you...homewrecker excuse #2 "He's not happy. They have problems."

When you go to McDonalds you know good and dang gone well there is a good chance that,

1. The ice cream machine is down.
2. You will need to ignore the cars behind you and check your order BEFORE you pull off because something is missing.
3. The fries are cold.
4. You don't have enough sauce for the number of nuggets you ordered.
5. You will have to pull ahead to "Space Number 1" if there is ANY variation in your order.
6. They are out of pies.
7. Ketchup comes in 2 levels of availability: None and One.
8. You will have to ask for their tightly rationed napkins one at a time until everyone who ordered has one.
9. If the sun is down no one is at Window 1 and the person at Window 2 is still trying to get the lid on your drink.

When you pull in **you know these things**, and YET you still go knowing there are going to be guaranteed problems! You weather the storm because you really – really want a Filet-O-Fish with extra tartar sauce and a slice of "almost cheese". Likewise, no one in their right mind should be getting married thinking there will never be problems. You go into it knowing that something, at some point will go wrong. It doesn't mean that it is a bad decision to go, it simply means you go in prepared to be a problem solver.

1. **No napkins:** Have some in the glove compartment
2. **Pull forward**: Sure, throw in a cookie for my inconvenience please.

3. **Ice Cream Machine is down**: FIX IT. I'll wait.

When you get married things are bound to come up. Difficulties do not mean getting married was a mistake and tough times do not give you the right to cheat. Neither do these excuses:

1. **Sex isn't exciting**: Keep practicing (Read books, get creative, talk through issues)
2. **Poor Communication:** Get counseling, restart date night. GET OFF YOUR CELL PHONES and TALK!
3. **Growing Apart:** Decide to recommit to growing together.

The reality is, if a man has no self-control or a close walk with God - he will cheat. That has nothing to do with his wife being a good person or bad person and ladies, if he will cheat with you, he will cheat on you.

As a hoe you need to understand, you are complicit in sin and the consequence will fall on you just like it was fall on the person you are sinning with. This is especially important for single homewreckers to understand. You are guilty of adultery if you interfere in someone else's marriage. If you don't want someone to mess with your spouse don't do it to someone else.

You don't have to be the married party to be an adulterer. If you are involved with anybody else who is married you are 100 percent, no-holds barred, no exceptions - WRONG. I don't care if they say:

1. I'm not happy
2. We're breaking up,
3. I don't live with her

4. I don't feel fulfilled,
5. It's not how it used to be.
6. I wish I would have met you first.
7. I'm only staying for the kids
8. Give me time, we'll be together.
9. If she treated me like you do I wouldn't be cheating.
10. I would never cheat on YOU.

All of those things do not matter! If somebody is married, they are married, and they are off limits to you. Don't think what you do will only impact you, it will impact generations of other people who may be directly and indirectly affected by the decision to interfere with a marriage. There are children impacted in many marriages and when you get finished having your 5,10, 20 minutes of pleasure you are going to impact the emotional stability of little lives and for that, you have blood on your hands.

Do you really think he's going to leave his family for you? Even if he left her for you my dear sister, you need to understand you will never be the hero of the story. When the kids ask, 'How'd you meet my dad', what are you going to say?

"Well, I was over here giving it out while your mama was at home cooking dinner, raising you, helping you with homework - he was laid up with me".

- Sister! Is that who God made you?
- Is that the depth of your character and your worth?

- How will you ever have peace with the man that you know will lie
  - because he lied to be with you?
- How would you have peace with a man who you know will cheat
  - because he cheated with you?

You will never lay with total confidence beside that man because you know what he's capable of and the same way he told you that she wasn't enough he'll tell the next hoe the same thing about you. Stop being a homewrecking hoe.

## The Church Prowling Hoe

The next hoe we're going to address is the church prowling hoe. The church-prowling hoe is the kind of woman that dresses up with half her clothes on and 10-inch heels to prance around during offering wearing no girdle, no pantyhose and no underwear trying to make sure her butt shakes and cups run over so every man sees her because if she can't have the pastor a deacon, trustee or choir member will do.

Yea, he sees you. We see you. The kids see you. The Mother's Board sees you – but do YOU see you? Everything about you says, "She'll do it all for two Happy Meals and a budget movie" Get it together. We are not impressed.  God calls for our modesty as women. The NBA has a dress code, the club has a dress code and BY GEORGE the church has a dress code!

No matter WHAT a woman has on or how she advertises Shepherds have no business sleeping with the sheep. Under no circumstances should leaders be having sexual relationships with **anyone** under their care; and, I'm not just talking about children.

**ANNOUNCEMENT: If you are in charge of somebody's spirit and they are under your leadership and you are in a position of power and authority over them, you ought not be sleeping with them. EVER!**

First, if you're not married, God knows you shouldn't be sleeping with them! You are doing the very thing *you ought not be doing* while you're preaching to them about what they *should* be doing. Whether they are volunteering to meet your sexual needs or not, you are being a bad example and you are leading them astray.

**"Jesus said to his disciples: "Things that cause people to stumble are bound to come, but woe to anyone through whom they come.  It would be better for them to be thrown into the sea with a millstone tied around their neck than to cause one of these little ones to stumble. <u>So watch yourselves</u>." Luke 17:1-3** (Emphasis mine)

That being said, we must address the fact that there are women who are coming into churches to find a man of God, and worse still - specifically targeting a preacher. Many are even seeking pastors because of what they think is the glamorous ~~is the~~ life of the First Lady.

Let me assure you that very few people understand the stress and the depth of responsibility it is to be the First Lady of a church. You have to hold things in confidence, become the automatic chairperson of this committee and that committee. You raise your children under the glare of an entire church who will criticize, critique, and make mention of their "concerns" passive aggressively. People will say things that will cause you to feel emotionally vulnerable and yet you still must be careful not to respond to foolish things and make yourself, your husband, your family, or your God look bad.

Nevertheless, there are women who are foolish enough to believe that the man that you see standing in front of you is perfect. You think that he always looks good and smells good. You think that his job is glory-filled and if you were with him you would be able to enjoy some of that glory. Baby, if you are out here trying to be a sexual distraction to the men of God at the cost of your dignity – you aren't ready to be a Christian let alone a First Lady. Being the First Lady is more than big hats, nice shoes and a seat in the front.

The reality is the man you see every Sunday is an imperfect person. It's just when you see them, they tend to be at their best. As they stand behind the sacred desk they are generally at a heightened place of prayer and reflection. They're dressed up and nine times out of ten, they're talking about love, forgiveness, redemption and peace...sexier words can't be found – especially if you are broken. Nothing drives a woman more insane than hearing a man talk about the redeeming power of love.

If that's not your husband, then you have no business sleeping with him but to turn around and try to play the victim once the relationship ends. To suddenly act tearful and vulnerable when you wake up and realize that after all you did, he has no interest in advancing the relationship – is not acceptable.

Whether you knew they were married and off limits, or when you knew that they were single but you were not married to them - you both were wrong and need to repent.

Yes, there are people who are taken advantage of, and I'm <u>not</u> speaking about those people. I'm talking about people who come in, eyes wide open with a made-up mind to cause problems. I've seen it.

**Men stop being flattered by the attention**! Her assignment was given by satan to destroy you and the ministry that you have been entrusted with. You liking her attention is the equivalent of winking and blowing kisses at your hitman! There are so many great leaders sitting at home on Sunday, with no marriage, ministry or plan for rebuilding wondering, "how did I end up here"? Many have looked at these women as "snacks" but rest assured they will give you indigestion because they <u>cannot</u> help you with your assignment and they are not help-meets! *mates*

- These are the kind of women who come in to size up the pastor's wife to see how much it would take to get this man distracted and looking at them instead of looking at her.
- These are the women who stay in pastors face for no reason and need private counseling every five minutes until you recommend that she talk to another woman on staff - then she's suddenly healed. Half of the reason we had to double down on adjutants and security is to keep the hoes moving and the pastor out of trouble!

The Church prowler is more subtle than the homewrecker. This is the woman who bakes the pastor a cake 'just because' - but hasn't baked her own husband one since his last birthday. The church prowler asks what the Pastor would like her to cook him for dinner, but never asks about his wife or children's culinary preferences. We see you; we may not say anything, but most times your meal sits politely on the corner of the desk until you pull off.

## We throw out more cake than a bakery around these parts!
**Don't waste the butter.**

You come to church, not to worship, not to praise, but to prowl and God sees you right where you are. You are not a new phenomenon beloved. The Bible declares that back in biblical times there were temple prostitutes. They had the same mentality. They came to the temple for one purpose: they wanted to get the men to give them offerings in exchange for sex acts under the illusion that once they had that moment of release they would be cleansed and be in a new place spiritually. It's still false and it's still wrong. **Don't go to church prowling for men.**

### The Hypocritical Hoe

The hypocritical hoe is the woman that judges' women who walk on the street and talk about how "it's a shame that they act that way and they do that" and "it's a shame that she's a prostitute". Yet you live your life manipulating men for money. You allow men to buy you things and when times get tough enough you will do "something strange for change". The reality is you are simply a hypocritical hoe.

You arrogantly judge another woman who is walking the street for 3, 4, 8 hours a night so she can feed her children because she's in a desperate financial, emotional, addiction-driven or psychological situation but you're sitting here in your right mind claiming to love God while you let this one buy your hair, another one buys your purses and yet another one pays other bills. You, my friend, are for sale. When a woman is for sale and providing emotional, physical, or sexual services for a fee - you're a hoe, period. Stop bashing other women who are in the same mess you are in. Get yourself together and help her as well. Either your heavenly Father is a provider or

He isn't. Every time you resort to these tactics you bring shame to the Body of Christ and make clear you do not trust God to meet your needs.

## Male Hoes.
## (...Everybody just hold still, I'll be to your row in a minute)

Now, male hoe's, I didn't forget about you. Men, you can be just as whorish (and significantly more so) as women. We tend to lecture our young women and our teen girls and make them feel like they are the sole person responsible for sexual purity in a relationship. We tell them over and over "make sure you say no, keep your legs closed, don't do this, and don't do that", but we'll look at our sons and say to them, "be careful, use a condom, don't get her pregnant." Not only should we teach our daughters to say no, we must teach our sons not to ask.

We cannot condone whorish men. We cannot condone men sowing their seeds all over the kingdom. We've got men with baby mamas and mistresses in multiple states that we still let get up, preach, teach, shout, direct and everything else in the church without correction or consequence. The devil is a liar! There has got to be a consistent standard because if a woman did the same thing – if a woman had baby-daddies in five different states you wouldn't even let her read scripture let alone fly her in to preach.

Ya'll know I'm not lying! She couldn't sing a solo until 2047 when she got her AARP card and y'all were pretty sure everything had dried up like Sarah. Again, I'm not saying that we should ostracize people for past mistakes. We ALL have made mistakes. The problem is when we chose to adopt the mistakes as an acceptable life style and keep serving with unclean hands as if we do not see the error of our ways. Where is the repentance? Where is the commitment to do better? Where is our accountability and process for restoration?

**There is still a standard for holiness!**

When men collectively reclaim the standard and realize that because you're not whoring around doesn't make you soft, gay or less of a man the Kingdom will be better. In fact, choosing to live holy despite temptation everywhere means you're a man that understands that destiny is more important than temporary pleasure. The same way you don't want some high mileage woman, some of us women don't want a man with a bunch of miles on him either. Don't be a male whore.

## The hoe in denial: So, you think you're not a hoe?

This is the woman who will read this entire chapter with her fornicating self and still doesn't see anything wrong with what she is doing. This woman goes to church but has a man and she says,

- All I do is sleep with my man.
- I only have one partner at a time, I'm not a hoe.
- At least I'm not like sister so-and--so.
- At least I'm not having a bunch of kids out of wedlock.

## You are the hoe in denial.

We all can make mistakes, but the worst kind of person is the person who can't own their mistakes and the church is becoming so politically correct that we won't just flat out tell people when they're wrong.

I'm fat. It is what it is. I'm cute, but I'm fat. So, here's the reality- when I walk my fat tail into the doctor's office, every time I go, the doctor tells me, "by the way, you do know you're fat right?" "Yes sir, I am aware." He then tells me, "you need to get this fat off you because although right now you don't have high blood pressure or diabetes, if you keep on this path eventually something bad is going to happen to you". Now when he tells me that, he doesn't know if I'm going to blow up, or cry, start ranting or tell him I'm never going to come back again - AND HE DOESN'T CARE.

**His job is not to guard my feelings,
his job is to tell me the truth and guard my body.**

As preachers and teachers of the word of God it is not about guarding people's feelings, it's about guarding people's souls. It doesn't matter if you are sleeping with one man that wasn't your husband or ten men that weren't your husband. Hell is hot no matter how you get there. We, as preachers need to get back on the wall, and get back to telling people the right thing versus the wrong thing. They can get mad, they can storm out, they can leave, hey, you can return my book but at least you heard the truth and the truth can't be unheard once you hear it. The moment you hear it, the moment you read it, you became accountable and you can never tell God, "I didn't know", "No one told me", or "My church didn't talk about that."

Baby you done messed around and read the chapter. Now you know, don't be a hoe

**Heaven and the hoes, there is good news.**

The Bible says that we can be forgiven and brought back into God's good graces no matter what we've done. Maybe you started this chapter and you were doing something crazy last night and you know this chapter is all about you and you want to be better. The good news is God still loves you.

God wants you to trust him to forgive you! Repent of that sin and tell him where you were wrong. There is nothing you are going to say that will shock Him and nothing you can say to make Him stop loving you or regret creating you.

Ask him to touch your heart and where you no longer even feel convicted by the things you do, ask Him to please make you feel convicted, so you have the desire to be different and the desire to be changed. The good news is that if you are reading this book, it isn't over and you can still go to heaven.

When you are sexually intimate with someone you can get a condom to cover your genitals but there is no protection available to cover your soul and some of the ways you may be feeling emotionally, spiritually psychiatrically etc., may be in part because you keep becoming one flesh with different people.

We have lived in a society now that is glamorizing your "body count" - how many people you have had sex with. What should worry people far more is your demon count! You might have slept with five people, but you might have come home with 17 demons and that is a problem in the kingdom that we are not addressing - the fact that there are consequences both natural and spiritual for our behavior.

I'm not under any delusion that we are all some perfect, sanctified, puritanical people. I am simply saying that we can no longer look the other way and act as though our sexual lives don't matter and our choice to continue living in a whorish state doesn't offend God, because it does. Even when we step back and look at the damage of our own making - God is faithful and just to forgive us if we simply ask. We can get a fresh start and a clean slate, and we can be who He wants us to be.

# CHAPTER 7:

## A QUICK MESSAGE TO THE PEDOPHILES AND PREDATORS

**Sadly, this is another issue that the Kingdom has failed to address properly.**

At the time of this printing 26 states have revised their reporting laws to include clergy as mandated reporters. Simply put, this means telling the police about abuse is not based on some subjective reflection you do in your office or with your board.

**You MUST call the police when a crime against a child has been committed.**

You may be asking why I am addressing this issue in a book on dating and "Boaz" not wanting "Ruth". For too long the world – including the church – has turned its collective head as adults rape children.

When you see the word 'pedophile' many times you think of someone lurking in a park salivating over the thought of a three-year-old. Sick right? Yes, it is sick and it should make all of us enraged. However, our collective stomach should turn just as much when we see a 25-year-old man with a 14-year-old girl or a 50-year-old with man a 16-year-old girl.

If you are a grown man and think, "as long as there is grass on the field, she's ready to play" you are a pedophile and a predator. You are wrong and society must stop normalizing this behavior. Stop making excuses!

- She's not mature for her age.
- It doesn't matter how she's built.
- It's still wrong if her mom knows.
- It's still wrong if she "initiates".

## SHE CAN NOT CONSENT TO SEXUAL ACTIVITY OF ANY KIND!

Unfortunately, more and more women are joining the ranks of the pedophile in their pursuit of young teen boys. Young men tend to see themselves as conquerors rather than sexual assault victims when an adult woman sleeps them. There are no exceptions for women who violate children. You are wrong too!

## BREAK THE CYCLE

The only way to stop this is to address it. We have to break the cycle. Perhaps someone hurt you. Maybe you are hurting someone. Get help and break the cycle.

# CHAPTER 8:

## JESUS WAS SINGLE: A FEW REMINDERS FROM THE SINGLES IN YOUR CHURCH

Every now and then I think it's helpful to issue some reminders to the church regarding singles.

**Singles have always contributed to the church!**

People tend to forget that those they quote most from regarding, love, marriage and divorce were both unmarried. Jesus was single and so was Paul. Just because someone is unmarried doesn't mean they can't support, love and when needed help people who <u>are</u> married.

**Everyone single is NOT on the prowl!** Please do not tell people that once they get married, they should not have single friends. Don't be fooled! I promise you there are plenty of married people you need to keep your eye on around your spouse!

**Single people have lives too!** Singles have the right to live and enjoy life just like married people. Do not assume single members of your church have "nothing else to do" simply because they are not married or do not have children. We do not want to serve on every committee. We are not "automatically free" to travel with you, the choir or the Mother's Board. The time of singles needs to be respected and balance encouraged.

**You are not more of an adult or more of a Christian because you are married**. PLEASE, married people, be careful how you talk to single people. Sometimes there is a level of condescension that is woven in conversation and at times even in sermons.  A single person can say they are tired and someone will chime in that tiredness for a single person is impossible – especially if they don't have kids. Rent is due when you are single, car notes are due when you are single, other bills are constantly coming when you are single – and there is no one to help pay them. There is no second check. There is no supportive backrub...they're working it out on their own. Don't speak to singles as though they aren't equals. Married people are not better than single people or vice-versa.

**We need continual, supportive ministry that isn't a meat market.**

After youth ministry concludes churches tend to have major gaps in programs that meet the real-life needs of members 21-35. It's no wonder this is the age where we tend to lose members! Singles need a safe place to meet, socialize and enjoy life that isn't hosted by married people saying, "come out, maybe you'll meet someone". The church is not a meat market – singles needs platonic friends too! The same effort you pour into marriage ministry, youth ministry, children's ministry and senior ministry needs to be replicated for the singles. The only group getting less love than the singles are the pets! You can't fail to provide an outlet for adult singles and simultaneously get mad when they create their own fun in places you don't approve of.

## CHAPTER 9:  SO YOU THINK YOU FOUND THE ONE!

Please enjoy this bonus copy of my
*Before you Even Ask (BYEA)*...pre-engagement counseling
questionnaire.

**We also have trained BYEA reps that can provide pre-engagement
services online**
CLICK **"Contact us"** on RevTeaches.com

# Before you even ask,...and before I say yes!

Pre-engagement Questionnaire - Written By: Pastor Roxanne Cardenas, M.Div.

1. What is your full legal name?

   _____

2. Have you ever had another legal name or alias?

   _____

3. When you were born, what gender were you?

   _____

4. Are you desiring to transition into any other gender **now or in the future**? _____

5. Are you currently married?

   _____

6. Have you **ever** been married?

   _____

7. Have you ever filled out a marriage license in any state, ever?

   _____

8. If you were previously married how, when and why did the previous marriage(s) end?

   How _____

   When_____

   Why

   _____

   _____

   (Please feel free to use additional paper.)

9. If you are divorced, was your divorce legally filed and legally finalized? _____

10. Do you have, and will you provide, the court documents with the affixed seals proving you are legally divorced?

_____

11. Have you ever been previously engaged? If so how many times? _____

12. If you broke a previous engagement, how many months/weeks/or days were you from the wedding date when the plans were canceled?

_____

_____

## Legal

1. Where were you born?

_____

2. What states have you lived in?

_____

3. What were the reasons you moved to and from these locations? (i.e. Jobs, college etc.)

_____

_____

4. Are you a U.S. citizen?

_____

5. Have you ever been arrested? If so, please explain.

_____

_____

_____

6. Have you ever been incarcerated, placed on probation or parole? _____

_____

_____

7. What were the charges and what was the legal disposition?

   _____

8. Are you a felon? _____

9. Are you a registered sex offender?

   _____

10. Have you ever been charged with a sexual crime although not on the registry? _____

11. Do you have <u>any</u> legal criminal or civil pending cases?

    _____

12. Do you have a living will or active power of attorney in place? _____

13. If so, will these documents be changed should we decide to get married?

14. Do you have a valid driver's license?

    _____

15. Have you ever lost your driver's license? If so, please explain

    _____

    _____

    _____

## Finances

1. How will you determine who handles the finances?

   _____

   _____

   _____

2. Do you know your credit score? If so, what is it?_____

3. Do you have bad credit? If so, why?

   _____

4. How will expenses be paid?

   _____

   _____

   _____

5. Do you want a pre-nuptial agreement?

_____

_____

_____

6. Will the accounts be separate or joint? Explain.

_____

_____

_____

_____

_____

7. Do you owe back taxes?

_____

            If so how much do you owe?

_____

            Do you have a payment plan with the IRS?

_____

8. Do you owe back child support? If so how much?

_____

9. Have you filed, or plan to file, bankruptcy?

_____

10. In an average month how much do you currently spend on:

    a.   Tithes/offerings

        _____

        _____

    b.   Clothes

        _____

        _____

    c.   Shoes

        _____

        _____

d. Hair/nails

_____

_____

e. Hobbies

_____

_____

f. Music

_____

_____

g. Entertainment

_____

_____

h. Rent

_____

_____

i. Car

_____

_____

j. Insurance

_____

_____

k. Child Support/Alimony

_____

_____

1. What standard of living do you currently have and what standard of living do you expect?

_____

_____

_____

_____

2. What do you consider success?

_____

_____

_____

3. What is your best financial habit?

_____

4. What is your worst financial habit?

_____

5. Do you have life insurance?

_____

   *Is the amount of life insurance that you have enough to cover all of your debts, your funeral arrangements and provide for your intended family for 3-5 years min.?

   _____

6. Who will be listed as the beneficiary should we decide to get married? _____

_____

_____

## Children
1. How many children do you have?

_____

2. Are there any children you could have possibly fathered that you are not aware of?

_____

_____

3. Have you been pregnant or gotten someone pregnant? What was the result of any pregnancies listed?

_____

_____

_____

_____

4. Do you want to have children, or additional children? If so, how many? _____

_____

_____

5. Do you have custody of any of your children?

_____

6. Do you have visitation with any of your children, if so, when? _____

7. Will any of your children be living with us?

   _____

8. Are any of your wages being garnished or otherwise surrendered for child support?

   _____Percentage

   _____%_____

9. In case of our disability or death who would rear our children?

   _____

   _____

10. Would you expect me to continue to rear or maintain visitation with children you had before our proposed marriage after your death?

    _____

11. How do you feel children should be disciplined?

    _____

    _____

    _____

    _____

    _____

12. What race will the children be considered?

    _____

    _____

    _____

13. What are you going to tell your children about race (skin color, hair texture etc.)?

    _____

    _____

## Medical History

1. Do you have any medical issues currently? (Allergies, reproductive, etc.) _____

_____

_____

_____

_____

_____

_____

1. Do you have any family medical conditions (genetics)?

_____

_____

_____

_____

_____

_____

_____

2. Do you have any medical problems that may prevent pregnancy? _____

3. Have you ever struggled with mental health issues, including depression? _____

4. Were you ever given a diagnosis, medication or therapeutic treatment plan? _____

_____

_____

5. Have you ever attempted suicide? If so, did you seek professional help? _____

_____

_____

6. Have you ever been depressed for an extended period of time (one month or more)?

_____What was the
outcome? _____

7. Has anyone in your family suffered from mental health
   issues? _____

_____

_____

_____

_____

8. Have you ever been seen, treated, or hospitalized for any
   mental health issues? If so, please explain.

_____

_____

_____

_____

_____

_____

9. Have you been tested for HIV? _____When and
   what were the results? _____ Have you had sex
   since that test?  If so, when will you be retested?
10. When was your last full medical work-up?

   _____

11. Have you ever been addicted to any substance (nicotine,
    alcohol, prescription, illegal or legal drugs)? If so, please
    explain.

_____

_____

_____

_____

## Emotions

1. How affectionate are you?
   _____

2. Do you feel public displays of affection are appropriate or
   expected? _____

   _____

   _____

3. How do you show love?
   _____

4. How do you want love to be shown to you?
   _____

5. How do you deal with stress?

   _____

   _____

   _____

   _____

   _____

6. Have you ever been in an abusive relationship?

   _____

   _____

   _____

   _____

   _____

7. What are the best 3 things about you? The worst?

   _____

   _____

   _____

   _____

   _____

   _____

   _____

_____

_____

_____

_____

_____

_____

8.  What are the best 3 things about your intended spouse? The
    worst? _____

_____

_____

_____

_____

_____

_____

_____

_____

_____

_____

9.  How will you respond if the **worst** attributes belonging to
    your intended spouse never change?

    _____

    _____

    _____

    _____

10. How many times have you been in love?

    _____

**Sexually Speaking**

1. When did you become sexually active?

   _____

2. Have your experiences with sex been generally positive or negative? _____

3. Approximately, how many partners have you had?

   _____

4. What is your view on oral sex?

   _____

5. Have you ever considered, experienced, practiced, or experimented with homosexuality in any form?

   _____

   _____

   _____

   _____

   _____

   _____

6. Have you ever had, or been a "friend with benefits"?

   _____

   _____

   _____

7. Have you slept with **anyone** I know or to whom I am related?

   _____

8. Sexually speaking, what type of person would you say is your most ideal match?

   _____

   _____

9. Are you open to trying new things sexually?

   _____

   _____

   _____

10. What are you absolutely not willing to do sexually?

    _____

11. In an average week how often would you want to be intimate with your intended spouse?

_____

12. Do you watch pornography?

_____

What type of pornography do you watch?

_____

13. Do you pay for pornography?

_____

14. Do you have any fetishes? (i.e. feet, bondage, etc.)

_____

15. Have you ever hired an escort/prostitute?

_____

16. Have you ever been an escort or prostitute?

_____

17. Have you ever been molested or otherwise sexually violated?_____

18. If so, when and by whom?

_____

19. How has this violation impacted you?

_____

## Family History

1. While growing up did you witness any instances of domestic violence in your household or immediate family?

_____

2. Were you reared in a one or two parent family?

_____

3. How did that impact you?

_____

_____

_____

_____

_____

4.  How is your relationship with your family of origin?
    (Mother, father, brothers, and/or sisters)

_____

_____

_____

_____

5.  Who will care for your elderly parents?

_____

_____

_____

_____

_____

6.  Do you like or have any pets? If so what kind?

_____

_____

_____

_____

_____

## Future Expectations

1.  Where do you see yourself in 2 years? 5 years? 10 years?

_____

_____

_____

_____

_____

_____

_____

2. Where will vacations be spent?

_____

_____

_____

_____

_____

3. Where will holidays be spent?

_____

4. Who will have keys to our home?

_____

5. How often do you host guests?

_____

6. How will household duties be accomplished?

_____

_____

_____

_____

_____

7. Do you feel that going out is important even after marriage? If so how often?

_____

_____

_____

_____

8. What are your political views?

_____

9. Can you vote? _____ Do you vote?

_____

## Religion

1. What religion are you?

_____

2. What God do you serve and what does your religion believe in **specifically**?

3. What church affiliation will we have?

_____

4. What church will we attend?

_____

5. What do you think God desires from you and from your life?

_____

_____

_____

_____ 6. What role do you expect me to play in what you believe God has planned for your life?

7. Did you seek the Lord in your decision to marry me?

_____

8. Is divorce an option for us?

_____

Made in the USA
Columbia, SC
04 August 2019